SPIRITUAL PRISON BREAKS

HOW TO RECLAIM YOUR STOLEN POWER

by
Bruce A. Miles & Evelyne Deleuze-Miles

Copyright © 2016 by Bruce A. Miles & Evelyne Deleuze-Miles

Spiritual Prison Breaks
How To Reclaim Your Stolen Power
by Bruce A. Miles & Evelyne Deleuze-Miles

Printed in the United States of America.

ISBN 9781498490528

All rights reserved solely by the author. The author guarantees all contents are original and do not infringe upon the legal rights of any other person or work. No part of this book may be reproduced in any form without the permission of the author. The views expressed in this book are not necessarily those of the publisher.

Scripture quotations taken from the Holy Bible, New International Version (NIV). Copyright © 1973, 1978, 1984, 2011 by Biblica, Inc.™. Used by permission of Zondervan. All rights reserved.

Scripture quotations taken from the King James Version (KJV)–*public domain.*

Scripture quotations taken from the English Standard Version (ESV). Copyright © 2001 by Crossway, a publishing ministry of Good News Publishers. Used by permission. All rights reserved.

The authors acknowledge www.Biblegateway.com for facilitating our many years of research and sourcing Bible verses through the use of their website.

www.xulonpress.com

Endorsements for
Spiritual Prison Breaks

In this book "Spiritual Prison Breaks", Bruce and Evelyne bring new understanding of how to dispel the lies of the enemy and break free from bondages and fears that keep us locked up.

We pray "Spiritual Prison Breaks" becomes part of your journey to freedom as you invite Jesus through the doors of your troubled past and allow Him to bring healing to you today, while establishing hope for a greater tomorrow.

As you read these pages you will be empowered to form godly beliefs, as the revelation of your identity in Christ is fully fashioned in you, through the establishing of "TRUTH".

Let the past...be the past as you learn to face, embrace and erase while reaching forward to the high call in Christ Jesus. Your past does not have to dictate your future. Let this book help you to let go of the old and embrace the new...God has for you!

Dr. Russ Moyer
Founder and President of Eagle Worldwide Ministries

Bruce and Evelyne have been helping set people from the captivity of generational curses, wounding from life's hurts, lies believed, and demonic oppression for years.

Now they have written a practical application on how to break out of spiritual prisons of the soul and spirit. The testimonies and stories of real life people who have received freedom are inspiring.

Bruce and Evelyne give practical steps on recognizing spiritual captivity and how to see breakthrough. Indeed, our God is the great freedom fighter. Bruce and Evelyne help us apply His principles of healing and liberty.

Rev. Patricia Bootsma
Co-Sr. Associate Pastor, Catch the Fire, Toronto
Director Catch the Fire House of Prayer
Leader of Ontario Prophetic Counsel

You hold in your hands a book of Faith, Hope and Freedom. Too many Christians are living a life trapped in prisons. Bruce and Evelyne have spent a lifetime teaching and equipping people as school teachers, and now as ministers of the Gospel, they have discovered the keys to unlock spiritual prison doors.

In their latest book, "Spiritual Prison Breaks," you'll discover real people breaking free of life bondages, giving hope that you can be set free as well. As you read, I pray faith arises in you, that strongholds of unwanted behavior and sin will be shattered as you apply the principles presented in this book.

What the body of Christ needs in this hour are mature men and women, empowered and equipped by the Holy Spirit, willing to go to the gates of hell to set the captives free. This truly is the Isaiah 61 ministry that Christ fulfilled and anointed us to proclaim.

Read the many amazing testimonies of spiritual transformation in this book. Your transformation is next. I highly recommend this book and the ongoing ministry of Bruce and Evelyne.

Rev. John Irving, MTS,
Senior Pastor, The Gathering Place, Aurora, Ontario,
Host, Great Lakes Outpouring, Aurora

Preface

We have seen amazing changes in people who have gone through the Spiritual Prison Breaking Process with us. It has brought new freedom and energy to frustrated individuals. We have seen the chains of fear and bondage broken to be replaced by confidence, hope and joy. We have seen the prisons of unworthiness shattered and true identity restored. What we have witnessed is beyond modern day Inner Healing and Deliverance. We are excited to share it with you. Jesus wants to free us from the grip of the evil kingdom. Jesus has defeated Satan. He is ready. We just need to call on Him to escape the life sucking lies of the evil one.

About the Authors

Evelyne and Bruce are Prophetic Prayer Ministers with the Healing House Network. They are cofounders of "You are God's Chosen Ministry." They have ministered to people from around the world and regularly see God transform and heal lives. Their ministry clients include pastors, ministers, missionaries, people of all ages and from all walks of life.

Their goal is to connect you with the Father's love and let Jesus heal your heart.

They are active members of Catch The Fire, Airport Campus, Toronto, Canada, and Eagle World Wide Ministries. They also belong to the International Coalition of Prophets.

For the past 12 years, Evelyne and Bruce have diligently pursued growth in healing and deliverance, through ministry, reading, prayer, conferences, and courses. They are happily married with children.

They are the authors of the amazing allegory called, "Meet the Secret Inhabitants of Your Mind." The book helps people "discover who you can trust in the battle for your soul."

Evelyne earned an honors BA in French and a B.Ed., and honed her ability to communicate simply and clearly over 28 years as an elementary school teacher in a multicultural urban center in Canada. Evelyne has been a presenter at workshops and conferences, including the Northeastern Regional Conference for Restoring The Foundations Ministries.

Bruce earned a BA in psychology and a B. Ed. He developed his sensitivity to challenged youth while teaching high school, special education, guidance, visual arts, and dramatic arts for over 26 years, and leading church youth groups for 25 years. Bruce earned a national award for authoring a conflict prevention and character building program, which was endorsed by the Toronto Police Services and the RCMP. Bruce was a presenter at the International Hate Crime Conference. He has served on many church boards and on the executive board of the Christian Businessmen's Committee in Ontario.

Bruce also earned an MBA in finance and marketing, which he used working as a Group Product Manager for multinational companies, managing a billion dollars in sales.

He was responsible for successfully launching five national products for companies, including Colgate-Palmolive and Kellogg Salada.

The authors can be reached at

Email **youaregodschosen@gmail.com**

Website **www.youaregodschosen.org**

The authors are available for exciting workshops. Feedback on the book is welcome.

Table of Contents

Preface		 ix
About the Authors		 xi
Chapter 1	What are Spiritual Prisons?	 17
Chapter 2	Spiritual Prisons of Fear and Bound Emotions	 26
Chapter 3	More Spiritual Prisons of Fear	 35
Chapter 4	Spiritual Prisons of Unworthiness and Shame	 42
Chapter 5	More Spiritual Prisons of Unworthiness and Shame	 50
Chapter 6	Spiritual Prisons of Sexual Bondage	 60
Chapter 7	Spiritual Prisons of Voicelessness, Hopelessness, Death, Anxiety	 66
Chapter 8	Spiritual Prisons of Sugar, Self, Neglect, Jealousy Rebellion	 74
Chapter 9	Testimonies	 83
Chapter 10	Procedure and Cautions in Ministry, Invitation for unbelievers	 95
Appendix	Bible verses referring to Spiritual Prisons	 101

Chapter 1

What are Spiritual Prisons?

We are really excited to share with you what Holy Spirit has shown us over the past four years. Many of God's people, unaware, are enduring horrible, Spiritual Prisons day after day, which keep them stuck, unable to embrace life to the full. The truth is Holy Spirit and Jesus want to help us get free from these life-sucking, demonic traps.

> **We believe we have received
> a new revelation about how to
> free people from spiritual prisons!!!**

In the day of the Inner Healing pioneers, around the 1980's, God showed John and Paula Sandford, how to see Spiritual Prisons that were holding people captive.

(Sandford, John and Paula, <u>Healing the Wounded Spirit</u>.)[1] More recently, Dr. Ana Mendez Ferrell in her book, <u>Regions of Captivity</u>,[2] describes how she saw her twin sister near death in a Spiritual Prison and was able to rescue her and subsequently many others from extreme prisons.

Both of these approaches rely on a gifted minister who can see into the spirit realm very clearly. Holy Spirit has turned the process upside down. Now Holy Spirit shows the person, who is captive in a Spiritual Prison, what their prison looks like, and they describe what they see to us. We, Prophetic Prayer Ministers, help them through the process. Jesus is the one who does the deliverance from the Spiritual Prison.

Why Are We Writing This Book?

We have seen amazing changes in people who have gone through the Prison Breaking Process with us. It has brought new freedom and energy to frustrated individuals. We have seen the chains of fear and bondage broken to be replaced by confidence, hope and joy. We have seen the prisons of unworthiness shattered and true identity restored.

---

[1] Sandford, John and Paula, Healing the Wounded Spirit, Victoria House, 1985

[2] Ferrell, Ana Mendez, Regions of Captivity, Jordan River Publishing, 2010 Pages ebook 306-372 of 1974

Who Should Read This Book?

Pastors who want to liberate their trapped sheep.
Ministers who seek to free others with inner healing and deliverance.
Individuals who struggle to become their best self, yet find their efforts are not enough.

Like a GPS

Spiritual Prison Breaks is like a GPS that helps pastors and ministers locate and destroy the Spiritual Prisons that have trapped their flock.

What Will You Find in This Book?

We will begin by exposing the truth about Spiritual Prisons. Next we will discuss the Legal System that governs the spiritual realm. We will present about 30 different cases of Spiritual Prison breaks relating to fear, unworthiness, rebellion, sexual bondage, hopelessness… for some, we will share their background. With others, we will focus on the actual prison break experience and their subsequent freedom, increased energy, more joy, fuller life…. We will also explain the Prison Break Procedure we have developed over the last four years.

Are Spiritual Prisons in the Bible? YES

Is it possible that David was referring to a Spiritual Prison in the following verse? He pleads with God to "Bring my soul out of prison, that I may praise Your name..." (Psalm 142.7 NIV). This passage shows that David was unable to bring himself out of "prison." David speaks prophetically, clearly showing us that our souls can be in a Spiritual Prison.

Is it possible that Isaiah and Jesus were referring to freeing people from Spiritual Prisons, not earthly prisons in the following verses?

> To open the blind eyes, to bring out the prisoners from the prison, and those who sit in darkness out of the prison house."
> (Isaiah 42:6,7 KJV)
>
> I will go before thee, and make the crooked places straight. I will break in pieces the gates of brass, and cut in sunder the bars of iron.
> (Isaiah 45:2 KJV)

It sounds to us like this prophecy declares Jesus will take us out of prisons.

More Bible references can be found at the end of the book.

Earthly Prison vs. a Spiritual Prison

Let's look at an earthly and a Spiritual Prison and make a comparison. In both cases, a breaking of a law has occurred, or been alleged. In both earthly and Spiritual Prisons, the court system has the power to incarcerate an individual who resides in their jurisdiction. In both systems the alleged guilty individual may or may not be responsible for the actions which gave legal rights to the judge to incarcerate. In both systems a pardon may be granted by a higher authority, such as a governor, president, Jesus, God. In both systems, the prisoner or a lawyer or legal defender or prayer minister may bring more evidence to help clear the prisoner.

The Heavenly Legal System

In our previous book, *Meet the Secret Inhabitants of Your Mind*,[3] we explained the spiritual legal system this way... "when our actions align with the kingdom of darkness, we give legal right to Satan and his demons to influence us. Alignment with the kingdom of darkness includes things like stealing, killing, lying, gossiping, hating, jealousy, and blame. When we do such things, we put ourselves

---

[3] Page 41, Miles, Bruce, Evelyne Deleuze-Miles, Meet the Secret Inhabitants of Your Mind, 2014

outside of God's protection and blessing, and we consequently are open to receive poverty, shame, disease, fears, and feelings of abandonment. As we follow one kingdom or the other, we give it permission to influence us in the legal way, just as if we signed a contract. There are legal rights or legal grounds that we either inherit or give up." (page 41)

Preparation to Get Free from a Spiritual Prison

In our ministry, we prepare the individual to get free from legal punishments from generational wrong beliefs and actions. With the help of God, the individual is able to form new godly beliefs and new godly identities, replacing the misconceptions from their past. They are also able to have their heart healed by Jesus from past hurts, and to forgive perpetrators from the pain they caused. We guide them in breaking the legal rights of demons to inflict emotional and physical pain and coach them in casting out demonic oppression. Next, we show them how to walk out their healing and to avoid giving legal rights to more demons who would bring oppression. But sometimes, in addition to all of this healing, individuals may still need a Spiritual Prison break.

What is the Difference Between a Soul Spirit Healing and a Spiritual Prison Break?

During a Soul Spirit Healing, Holy Spirit identifies a painful memory that He knows should be healed next. We lead the individual to be in touch with the pain of that memory. (In horrible traumatic memories, we gently touch on the memory, only enough to identify the pain. We do not force the person to re-live disgusting and degrading memories.) The individual invites Jesus into the memory, gives their pain to Him and asks Him to heal their heart. (We recommend Soul Spirit Healing for everyone.)

In a Spiritual Prison break, Holy Spirit shows the individual a prison in which a "piece of their soul has been legally captured and stuck there". Holy Spirit may slowly or quickly reveal to the person the different features of the prison. Soon the individual sees himself in the prison, and usually wants out. The individual then calls on Jesus to free him/her from the prison.

Author's Note: We are referring to "The Holy Spirit" as "Holy Spirit" because He is the third person of the Trinity, just as we don't refer to "Jesus" as "the Jesus." We have grown into this usage over time and we hope that you will be okay with our more personal usage.

The Difference Between Soul and Spirit

As you know, humans are made up of three key parts, spirit, soul, body. Our soul includes our mind, our will, our emotions, and our heart. Our spirit is that part which grows under the leading of Holy Spirit, which in turn is to lead our soul. Since most of us are unable to give 100% of our being to Jesus, it is possible for our soul to be fractured and broken and pieces of it held in captivity by the demonic world. You will see in the following examples that Jesus releases people's broken soul-pieces, heals them, and puts them back into the person thereby providing additional freedom to the individual.

How Do You Know When You Are in a Spiritual Prison?

If you have had inner healing and deliverance for the following issues and you are not feeling free, you may be in a Spiritual Prison.

1. You feel lonely but have friends.
2. You lack the energy to do something you want to do.
3. You are very critical of yourself.
4. You think God cares for others more than you.
5. You get some healing but seem to need it over and over.
6. You find it difficult to concentrate on your Bible reading.

7. Your talents and giftings appear out of reach.
8. You feel lost inside, but your life appears together.
9. You have trouble forgiving others who have hurt you deeply
10. You get really angry over small things.
11. You find it difficult to stay awake when you want to.
12. You find it difficult to sleep.
13. You worry over little things.

Authors' Note: If you have experienced extreme abuse, SRA, DID, psychotic episodes, witchcraft, PTSD, trauma etc. …we encourage you to seek ministry from a professional organization that specializes in your situation.

Chapter 2

Some Spiritual Prisons of Fear

Authors' Note: In order to protect the privacy of our clients, we have changed their names, their situations, and have left out any identifying clues as to their identity. Any similarity to persons living or deceased is purely coincidental.

Most humans will experience fear in some form or another. Fear can begin in the womb before the child even enters the world. The child may hear his parents fighting, or arguing over whether they want to keep him or her alive. We may experience fear of rejection, fear of lack, fear of poverty, fear of being a victim, fear of isolation, fear of failure, fear of success, fear that past failures will repeat...

This is Chad, a 35-year-old professional young man in a Spiritual Prison

Early in his life, fear came in as Chad's parents were working long hours away from home. He eventually went to live with his 'mean and critical' uncle. Chad became anxious over his educational performance. He feared being judged as unworthy. In order to protect himself from further shame, he chose lying to avoid the pain and rejection of criticism. While he felt the rejection of his real self, rebellion came and captured a piece of his soul. He became angry and bitter at his uncle's constant criticism on how he was to live his life.

> *I am running in an incredibly vast forest.... it's dark, trees are huge. I am naked. I am brighter than what's around me. It's like I'm glowing. I feel I am being hunted. I have been made to be brighter, like light comes out of me. I am lit up so people or things can easily see me. I'm constantly running from a 100-foot-tall giant monster who wants to eat me and hurt me. I'm tripping over things as I run. Each fall is painful as the ground is covered with sharp plants.*

There is a cage around me. It follows me wherever I go, but it won't protect me in any way. It just keeps me from climbing up trees. I'm tethered to the center of the cage. The creature can get me through the bars. The fear is that even if I eluded this one, the other monsters would force me back. I'm tired but I must keep running, I'm exhausted. Running and running and running. I live in terror. All my mind can think of is running to get away.

Giant birds are watching and swooping in on me. The ground is cold and wet. My feet slip and fall. I scramble to get up in the muck. My feet are hurting, my hands and knees are raw. The plants attack me as I go by. My eyes are hurting. I can't rest or I will be caught. Smaller animals are toying with me... giant birds are watching and swooping in, scaring me into different directions.

I invite Jesus into this prison. Jesus comes. He stands there as a tall figure. I'm stooped on my knees. I feel a shield of protection around us. Nothing can get in. There is peace and quiet; I know it's different. I close the door of the prison; it shatters into pieces.

> *I gave Jesus the piece of my soul to clean that had been trapped in this prison of fear. This piece of soul looked like a shard of light brown pottery. I gave it to Jesus. It became like soft flesh. He put it back into my abdomen. He put it right back into its place. It felt like it belonged in me. I am at peace and no longer afraid.*
>
> *There is another hole I see in my abdomen, but I don't know what it is.*

We suggested that Chad ask Holy Spirit about it. Holy Spirit told Chad that this hole was a result of his free-will being used to turn his back on God. His free-will chose to sin even though God was reminding him and prompting him not to sin.

Chad admitted...

> *I chose to sin anyway. I knew it was wrong and I was sorry. I repented for willful disobedience. I asked forgiveness and broke all agreements that I had made with demons. I renounced my alignment with the evil kingdom and pledged my allegiance to Jesus... to be upright, honest and not to follow the*

demons of control and rebellion as my operating platform. I asked forgiveness and laid down my willfulness at the cross.

This time the piece of my soul that had been imprisoned looked like a round cylinder, like a soup can on the ground. There was a big shower of water splashing all over my body. I moved my feet to make sure that the water would get under my feet. The hole was still in my body. The piece of soul was still on the ground. Jesus cleaned it until it looked good and then He put it back into the hole in my solar plexus. It felt like a key. He locked it into place. It became like a button...it turned me back on, activating me. I became more alive; I was connected to the power source- Jesus. My energy is coming from Him, no longer from myself. I mean I am powered by Jesus, like a lifeline.

I feel good, I feel lighter. Now I am 'ON.' I can live now. I feel like I am plugged in.

The Story of Greg and his Prison Breaks

Greg appeared to be a kind and gentle young man, hopeful to receive some healing. Unknown to Greg, he was in three Spiritual Prisons: fear, death, and bound emotions. Let's go back to his beginning and see what happened.

It turns out that Greg's father rejected him and neglected him. Greg felt fatherless and realized that there was a lack of intimacy and nurturing in his life. He began searching for a safe place, but he didn't find one. Greg was bullied at school through most years. When he got up enough courage to have a girlfriend, she rejected him. Greg became overcome by shame, focusing himself on the loss of himself and the shame from not being connected with his father, shame from feeling inadequate.

Shame paved the way for fear because when we feel shame, we want to hide it from other people. We are afraid they'll discover that there is something wrong with us, so we hide ourselves, hoping people will not find out who we believe we are.

Greg avoided being real. He was fearful of relationships because he didn't want to risk rejection. Greg had experienced some traumatic near-death experiences when he was small, which fueled fear in him. In addition, in his teenage years, there were times when people drugged his drinks and his health was put at great risk. As he grew, the feelings of bitterness and hopelessness entered and he began to resent his life. He was bitter about the way things were. The hopelessness just made room for more fear of the future. Being afraid of the future caused Greg to worry constantly. His mind would race and he couldn't sleep.

Greg tried to get help from God but God appeared distant. He started to doubt God. He prayed, but didn't see his prayers being answered; all of this set the stage for the need to find a way out of the pain. Greg realized that he was in a prison of fear. He couldn't sleep at night. He was afraid his life would turn out miserably. Greg hid his emotions so people would not make fun of him for being so afraid.

Holy Spirit showed Greg a prison of bound emotions. He saw words that seemed to have legs, with large letters, such as "joy," and "peace" walking in the prison. He invited Jesus to come into the prison. Jesus went into the prison; His light caused the bars to blow up, the prison was opened, and the emotions walked out of the prison, free at last.

Greg reported afterward that he was feeling much better about expressing himself, enjoying his emotions and that he felt more human.

Next Greg Dealt with the Prison of Fear

The prison of fear was very dark. In this prison, monsters were attacking his mind and his will constantly. Jesus went into the prison. Perfect love cast out Greg's fear. The walls burst and the prison of fear blew up.

There was a fear of the past that was still in darkness; the fear of things reoccurring. Jesus came and vacuumed up the past. He said, "What the Son sets free, is free indeed."

Greg said,
> I saw Jesus with me as a child, walk out of the prison; I slammed the door shut. I saw Satan try to put me back into the prison. Jesus hit Satan in the face. Jesus said I needed to walk out of the prison with Him. I saw myself jump into His arms. Jesus was holding me. I saw Satan in prison with the spear in him.

The prison of death was still holding a piece of Greg's soul.

> The prison of death was blackness like a fog trying to cover me. I couldn't see anything. Then I saw the light of Jesus as He entered into the room. When I repented and invited Jesus in, Jesus said, "let your light shine; the light penetrates the darkness." Jesus protected me.

Kelly and the Prison of Fear

Kelly was emotionally abandoned by her parents. Anxiety and the fear of the unknown developed in her. She felt the pressure of her parents for perfection, and tried to gain their approval by being perfect in everything she did at school. She chose to be voiceless rather than risk making mistakes in front of others. She realized others had more love from their parents and that she could never please her parents.

> *I was in a prison cell with monster bullies on the stairs preventing me from escaping. It was very dark and underground. They knocked me down each time I tried to come up. I hurt even more from falling on the rocks and stairs.*
>
> *I called on Jesus to lead me out, and He did. I closed the prison door forever. He washed the imprisoned piece of my soul and put it back in my heart. I felt a big sense of peace.*

Chapter 3

More Prison Breaks from Fear

Cynthia and the Prison of Fear

At about the age of five, Cynthia was accidentally locked in a closet in her house for about four hours until her grandfather discovered her. The trauma of this imprisonment scarred her for the rest of her life. It wasn't until Jesus broke her out of this prison that she was able to find freedom and joy in life. Here is how Cynthia described her experience.

> *I am walking in a field. I see a wall. I am wearing a black veil; the wind is sucking me into a hole. It drags me into the hole by forces I cannot control. I am terrified of being in there. I know when I am in there everything is black. There is not one beam of light. I try*

to resist so I will not be sucked into the long, narrow hole.

It is difficult to breathe. Particles are going into my nose. The smell of cement is suffocating and going into my lungs. Some ceiling holes are dripping water. I feel the slimy water on my feet; the water is gross. I am stuck in fear, I don't want to move, it is so repulsive...

I ask Holy Spirit if there's anything else He wants to show me? Holy Spirit says it is all fake, like card-board.

I see Holy Spirit taking apart the prison. I see the blood of Jesus running down a huge tunnel cleaning my piece of soul.

I realize that my fear was all a lie. Nothing but a trick of the enemy.

Phillip's Prison Break from Fear

In Philip's situation, it was the words of other people that put him in a prison and not his own misbehavior. As James asks in the Bible, who can tame the tongue?

> "... but no human being can tame the tongue. It is a restless evil, full of deadly poison."
> James 3:8 ESV

Philip's prison shows the power in the spirit realm that words can have over us.

> *I am in a corner of a cell, hiding and afraid to move. There are little snakes. Fear is connected to words about me. I see words on the walls that people said about me, spoken against me and about me. I fear what others say and think about me. I am tormented by the voices against me. It is dark, in a cave, stairs going up to the door. I was afraid to be loved, even by Jesus.*
>
> *I repent and ask Jesus to take me out of this prison of fear, Jesus takes me out.*
>
> *I see the burning fire of His love, burning the fear that I felt. I feel his burning love destroy the power those words held over me all my life. I feel his fire warming up my heart, I feel his light on my face.*

Samuel's Prison of Fear

Samuel was a 50+ year-old businessman who had been quite successful. But recently he had received many setbacks and seemed to be stuck, not going anywhere.

I see an open field with some trees, scattered trees, outdoors, may be like in Africa. A bunch of men with painted faces, wearing only loin-cloths... all pointing spears at me, standing in a circle. I'm only about 5 or 6 feet from the closest spears. There's probably a couple of hundred men with spears and painted faces. I can't really see their faces. They look very angry and ugly.

If I move, I will go into a spear because they keep jabbing them towards me. I stay put so that they don't hurt me.

... looking to see if I'm bleeding, I can't tell, I just know it's better not to move. I'm terrified, standing up in the middle of all of these spears.

The men are big and strong... they are like African warriors. I hear them chanting, "kill Samuel," over and over. The guys have formed an uneven circle around me and there's no way out. There seems to be slimy stuff on their spears, hanging off, could be poisonous...

I confess and repent for allowing myself to be immobilized by fear. I invite Jesus to come in to this prison. The men are parting; Jesus walks through them and reaches for my hand. He leads me out.

I close the door permanently to this prison, even though it's not a real door. I give the piece of my soul to Jesus to heal... I see the soul starting to glow and I praise Jesus.

I feel excellent, energized, like a weight has been lifted; I'm freer to move. I can go anywhere right now.

With the help of the prayer ministers, I was able to realize that I was holding an ungodly belief that said... "it is safer to do nothing." I asked Jesus for the truth. Jesus gave me a godly belief that said... "I am victorious in Christ." I adopted this godly belief as my own. As I repented for allowing fear to control me, God blessed me with boldness and courage.

Jessica's Prison of Fear

Jessica's father was a volatile, angry man who wanted a boy, not a girl. Jessica's father would yell at her, be angry with her over nothing and then apologize. This cycle was repeated day after day after day. You might think Jessica could turn to her mother for support, but sadly, her mother was so needy, she left Jessica alone and never defended her against her father.

Eventually Jessica started thinking something was wrong with her. She got the idea that if she had been really worthy, her father wouldn't have to get angry with her and her mother would really like her.

Fear grew and grew inside of Jessica, as her dad's outbursts became more and more violent. Out of fear, Jessica began to shut down and do everything in her power to avoid his explosions. She faced emotional abuse, mental abuse, physical abuse, verbal abuse and trauma on a regular basis. She became unable to trust boys or her father. She had no one to talk to and so she stuffed her emotions inside. Jessica could not be herself at school because in being the smartest in the class it would cause her to be rejected. So she couldn't be herself at home or at school.

With our help and encouragement, Jessica decided to confront the prison fear. As she describes it...

> *I'm sitting in a corner on the floor. There is a dark blue light. Some big demon blocks my way out. I am screaming to get out. I am hearing words said against me. They say I am worthless, I'm worthless. Over and over.*

I invite Jesus to come into this prison with me. Jesus comes in and cleans out the place. He throws the demon out. He turns a light on, flowers start growing out of the walls, Jesus tears down the walls and flattens them. Jesus stands and dances with me in a place like a field, very nice.

I had the revelation that Jesus deeply loved me and that I was precious in His eyes. The painful words spoken by others, and the inability to please my father all lost their power over me.

Although Jessica had lived a very pure and kind life, Satan still targeted her, to try to stop her from achieving her destiny.

Chapter 4

Spiritual Prisons of Shame and Unworthiness

A person in shame and/or unworthiness, often from wounding as a child, believes that there is something inherently wrong with them. Suffering from shame and unworthiness, the shameful child or adult believes that others are superior to them, that they do not have the same worth as other human beings. This condition is different from the concept that "oops I made a mistake," which is fixable. Real shame and unworthiness is severe damage to the soul. The person feels they are defective and will never be worthy, like others. They often become trapped in a shame-fear-control stronghold. While trying to hide their shame from others, they become fearful that others will see their "real horrible self." Consequently, they determine to control their environment and exposure so that they will not be found out to be less than others.

Crystal's Prison of Unworthiness

Crystal was emotionally abandoned as a child growing up. Neither parent had time for her. At the age of nine, she was sent to live with and look after her grandmother. Her grandmother abused her verbally and never had a good word for her. Crystal felt worthless, unloved, alone...

> *I see a vision of myself lying on the ground as a cadaver; my body has holes and sores; it has been eaten away all over. It feels like there is no life in that body, no energy to get up... looks like a dead body, but not really dead... looks like no one is around. Sores and holes are happening on their own.*
>
> *I see figures, people dressed in black, from head to toe, just moving around, talking to each other, looking at me with scorn and laughing and snarling at me.*
>
> *In desperation, I gather enough strength to call on Jesus to come and save me from this prison of unworthiness.*

Jesus comes quickly in an ambulance. I get a blood transfusion with Jesus' blood.

Jesus leads me out of the prison, where, I give the imprisoned piece of my soul to Him. Jesus washes it with his blood, and puts it back in my chest.

Jesus says that I am to go to Him often to get strength. My lifeline is tied to Him. I need to be more aware... spend time with Him more often. I said, "Thank you Jesus."

My ministers helped me to realize that I was holding onto and suffering from an ungodly belief which gave legal rights to the demons to keep me in the prison.

The false belief was, "I do not belong. I'm alone."

Jesus revealed the truth to me that I am created with a purpose in God... that I have a huge destiny before me. I am not alone. God has supplied everything I need to perform it; He is at my side.

With my newfound freedom, I was able to listen to God and to receive the blessing of an "abundant life."

Travis' Prison of Unworthiness

The pain of unworthiness and shame may be relieved temporarily by addictions. However, the feelings of hopelessness, despair, value through performance, deception, inconsistency, and lack of respect for self, all require healing to be resolved.

Travis describes his prison...

> *I am sitting on what looks like a demonic water slide. I can only really see the part where my back is and my feet. There is water coming from behind me. It's like the whole prison is carved out of rock. Water comes out of the hole about 10 feet above me and behind me. It's pretty dark. The water is echoing; its noise is painful to the ears.*
>
> *The waterfall tries to get me to slide down this slide into a big pool below that has two very ugly demons. I don't want to go down; it's a constant battle to keep up, and I no longer can stand. I am sitting, pushing back with my feet and moving my arms trying to hold on to the sides... I am trying to keep from falling*

down and being swept away by the powerful rush of water.

It is a constant struggle. I'm seated; my goal is to stand but I am unable. I can see the two creatures at the bottom of the slide... they seem to be excited that they will soon be devouring me. So I am terrified to go down there. It takes all my energy to keep where I am on the slide. If I could only stand up, I might be able to run away, but there is no way out.

I invite Jesus to come into this prison. The water stops. Jesus is there, standing, helping me to stand up and we walk out of the prison together. I kicked it down and closed the door permanently. I handed my soul to Jesus. He blew on it, made it dry and wiped it with His hand and put it back into my chest.

I feel good, really good. Not being able to stand was a helpful image. It let me see I have not been standing, having allowed myself to take a backseat. That's not what I was intended for.

Jesus made me aware that I needed to change the ungodly belief that, "I am unworthy to stand in my rightful place." He emphasized that in Christ the truth is that, "I am a respected ambassador of God's kingdom and I am worthy." Thank You Jesus

Travis reported to us a few months later that he had begun a small Bible group in his church.

Susan's Prison of Shame

Susan, now in her 40s, had had a lifetime of suffering when she came to us. Susan had been ridiculed her whole life by her parents, friends, teachers and bosses. She was afraid to look at people and always had her head down. She was so full of shame that she was unable to have any positive friendships.

In Susan's prison, she saw herself at a very young age, holding onto tall, thick, metal bars. She was helpless and alone with no one to even talk to.

Susan invited Jesus to come and free her from the prison. Let's listen as she describes it...

Jesus appears to me as The Lion of Judah[4]. He is gentle, yet fierce. His long, huge paw

---

[4] [4] Susan's image of Jesus as a lion is found in **Revelation 5:5 NIV** Then one of the elders said to me, "Do not weep! See, the **Lion of** the tribe **of Judah**, the Root of David, has triumphed. He is able to open the scroll and its seven seals."

> *lifts me up… He covers me in His mane. I am sitting, enjoying being in the softness of His mane. When I close the prison door, I am flooded with the glorious powerful light of Jesus' resurrection. Jesus, now appearing as a man, washes the piece of my soul and puts it back. I feel I have more freedom and the right to make my own choices.*

Susan reported back to us a few months later that her whole life was improved. She was able to stand up for herself many times at work. She became a respected voice at her church, and was establishing positive relationships with her family. She said that the prison break had permanently changed her life for the better.

Tiffany's Prison of Unworthiness and Shame

Tiffany was so full of unworthiness and shame that she had willingly put herself into a prison.

> *In this prison I am really little. It's not totally dark because there is some light from an opening, perhaps a window. I am alone, quiet, not scared, stuck there, feeling nothing, just stuck standing there. I am a kid, not doing*

anything, just looking at the window. I don't feel lonely. There is no door to get in or out. I think I allowed myself to be put here... I'm all alone. It is very quiet; the light is becoming brighter. I have imagination, so I'm not lonely.

There are noisy, ugly demons contained inside cages, who can't get out. They are not happy. I am in isolation in a big room, like a dungeon with low ceilings, and bars; light is way, way up high. I don't know why but I feel safe here.

I feel the presence of Jesus. I tell Him I don't want to leave. I feel safe here. I don't want to be outside. Jesus tells me that I must leave this prison. I say, "No, I don't want out." Jesus says, "Yes you do." I give Jesus permission to unblock my blocking. I give my feelings to Jesus, all the nervousness, all the exposure, the discomfort, the vulnerability around people, the need to hide, and the isolation. Jesus leads me out of the prison.

A few weeks later, Tiffany reported that she was comfortable talking with friends and acquaintances. She had much more energy and was much happier.

Chapter 5

More Prison Breaks from Shame and Unworthiness

Joshua's Prison of Unworthiness

Long before Joshua was born, his ancestors were participants in and victims of violence. He came into the world with his father beating his mother, with both of them suffering from trauma. Both parents chose to neglect Joshua's development. The normal security, encouragement and affirmation were not there, but were replaced by rejection, shame and unworthiness. Joshua grew angry at the situation and became bitter towards his dad, who refused to play with him or spend any time with him. He was sexually molested. He was bullied at school. His dad left home adding to his sense of shame. When he became a teenager, Joshua soon learned to please people in order to gain value, while still feeling very unworthy.

> *I could see that I was in a concrete block prison cell. The walls were black... and very thick. The room was about the size of a small office. It was peaceful. There was a small table with glasses and a pitcher of water on it.*
>
> *I was all alone feeling emptiness in my heart. I had given up my freedom, for a sense of safety where no one could hurt me again. I realized that I had to get out of here if I was to feel alive again.*
>
> *I asked Jesus to come in and free me.*
>
> *He came and led me by the hand out of the prison. I had always been afraid of Jesus, thinking that He was very unapproachable. But with me, Jesus was informal. He used the water pumped from the ground to wash the piece of my soul that had been trapped in the prison. He gave it back to me and put it into my heart. Jesus was smiling at me. The piece of my soul had a blue-color. It was about the size and texture of a handful of pastry dough.*

Joshua told us a month later that he had far more peace, was able to read the Bible for longer periods of time and get more out of it.

Doug's Prison of Shame

Doug came to us as a young man having difficulties in everyday living. He found himself lying to his boss and to his wife. He was full of lust, engaging in pornography, and being very self-centered. He was distraught over this because he thought of himself as a practicing Christian.

When Doug was small, his mother died in an accident. His father never really recovered from it. Doug found himself neglected, abandoned, and very much alone. His father never talked to him about his mother's death. He felt the effects of rejection and lack of intimacy, and ended up in loneliness.

Doug felt shameful and unworthy, never receiving his father's affirmation. It seemed that he could never measure up and this lead to a lot of guilt and inferiority, along with self-accusation, self-condemnation and self-hate. Without realizing it, his father put school performance as a priority. Doug adopted lying as a survival mechanism to avoid the pain of rejection and criticism. He became alone and voiceless. About the age of 12, Doug discovered pornography, which gave him some pleasure. He tried to stop it, but was unable.

Doug hid this from his wife, but found himself suffering from depression, discouragement, despair and suicide fantasies. He began to doubt God more and more. Despite a loving wife and a good job, Doug was persisting in self-destructive behaviors. He tried many things to correct himself but became angry at God because God was not helping him to get well.

Let's hear how Doug experienced his prison...

> *I see myself stretched out naked on the concrete floor with a spotlight on me. I am being held by ropes. There are crowds of people around, laughing at me; I can't move. There is no way to cover my eyes or my body. I cannot get away.*
>
> *I hear a voice recounting the shameful things that I have done. All the bad things are being repeated over and over. I am unable to cover my ears to prevent myself from hearing it. I can't hide anywhere. I am trapped.*
>
> *There is a giant screen in front of me. I am being forced to watch all the bad things I've done. I am helpless; I am laughed at*

constantly. Everyone I've ever known is there watching me doing all the horrible stuff I have done or said or lied about. They are forced to watch me. My shame is multiplied.

I ask Jesus to come in with ministering angels. I see the angels come and cut the ropes holding me. I am pronounced free in the name of Jesus. I close the door to the prison of shame never to go back. I offer to Jesus the piece of my soul that was in this prison and needs washing. Jesus washes the piece of soul with His blood. Jesus puts it back in my chest where there was a hole. I feel complete. The hole is not there anymore. The hole had been allowing cold air to flow back and forth to my body. Now, I'm slowly warming up again.

Doug and his wife together reported that Doug was a changed man since his Spiritual Prison break. He had stopped lying, had more energy, was able to apply enthusiasm to his work and was sleeping better.

Tammy's Prison Break from Criticalness and Judging

Tammy found that she was subject to the constant stream of judging other people and being critical of them.

She could not seem to shake this approach to life. She came by it honestly. Her father always had to be right. He instilled in her the sense of self-righteousness. Tammy became offended easily and was scared about many things. She was envious and jealous of what others had, and found it difficult to bless other people.

Tammy was overcome with bitterness, accusation, complaining, and resentment. The critical spirit caused her to blame her kind husband, even though she didn't want to. She found herself wishing bad things on other people. She was angry at herself and all others. She wanted God's mercy, but just for herself and not for others... even though she knew that was wrong. She wanted God to fix her, without her having to do anything. She kept blaming God for not fixing her right away. Tammy trusted no one, not even God. She thought everyone was going to betray her. She felt that God spoke with other people but not to her.

She believed that God punished her by making her fail exams, or by taking away her jobs. She was complaining that God was not working mightily in her life as she expected.

Because her parents wanted a boy, she experienced rejection and identity issues from her early years.

Her constant self-condemnation resulted in suicidal thoughts and self-hate. She believed that God could not have any good thoughts about her.

Tammy was unable to forgive herself for her mistakes. She could not forgive others for hurting her.

Tammy was in a prison. As she grew, she discovered she was becoming manipulative, like her mom. Tammy wanted to be comfortable with her body but she could not. She would often get overwhelmed at work. She didn't take vacations. She and her husband grew apart. Tammy encountered injustice at work which made her even more upset with God because she felt He was not looking after her. She became jealous of others who were happy. She wanted to be happy like them but instead, Tammy engaged in self-pity and self-condemnation.

Tammy's basic personal belief was that I am not worthy. I am shameful. Tammy felt a great sense of loneliness all the way through school and into her working life. Her husband didn't seem to be able to comfort her as she had hoped. Tammy kept thinking that her husband cared more for his friends and family than for her.

Tammy describes her prison

> *I see myself in a prison where the wallpaper has lips on it... talking all the time about others and about me. I am in the middle of the room down on my knees. I am holding my*

hands over my ears. The voices are constant. There is a tube to an outside wall into another room. There's a guardian, sitting on the chair. He moves to the left; I can see his profile. He's not looking towards me.

There are stones with water running between them, from the walls to the middle of the cell. It is hot and very humid. There are drops falling from the ceiling. I see a picture of me decapitated... I gasp in horror! I can see the outcome of self-hate.... Shaking, I invite Jesus to come into this prison. I see a dove coming over my head, coming down. It gave broken pieces of my soul to Jesus to heal.

Tammy shared sometime later that she is growing into a new freedom in being with other people. Her mind no longer judges every little thing and gradually her criticalness is turning into patient acceptance. As a result, Tammy is enjoying her time at work and with her husband, much more than ever before.

Shannon's Prison Break

Shannon appeared as a very competent young lady in her 20s. Her parents divorced early on in her life. Her dad did not really ever see her. He was distant, angry, and never complimented her. He lived with different women, but did not acknowledge her.

Her mom was cold, angry and bitter. Both parents had wanted a boy. Shannon became a tomboy for a while, to try to make them happy. That didn't work. Her sense of unworthiness and shame caused her to run after men who would simply dump her, which only magnified her feelings of unworthiness and of abandonment. She tried alcohol and drugs. She felt helpless in her situation. She couldn't see that her life was ever going to get better. Shannon was plagued by the fear from unworthiness, that she would look stupid and people would laugh at her. She expected friends would leave her and that if people ever got to know her, that they would not like her and leave her anyway.

She battled addictions of food, drugs and alcohol, sex, porn and smoking. Despite her feelings of shame and unworthiness she had embraced God, and saw the truth about living. However, she still had difficulty reading the Bible and she realized something was wrong.

Shannon realized she was in a prison of shame... that a piece of her soul had been captured in the evil kingdom.

Shannon Describes her Prison of Shame and Unworthiness

I can see myself. I am naked; it is dark. There are creepy creatures biting me all over, pulling on parts of my body with their teeth. They are speaking foul words and curses over me and jumping on my head.

There are hand-written letters all over my body. They were peeling them off. They were burning. They were words of people who had been saying bad things about me. Some creatures are scratching my skin constantly. There was an animated wolf with dirty gray-blue fur. The wolf represented the ancestors of both sides of my family. It spoke curses over me day and night.

I invited Jesus to come in. He healed my wounds and scars and crushed the demons. Jesus hugged me until I felt peace.

Shannon reported that she felt new freedom and a release of energy. She said she felt like a new person.

Chapter 6

Spiritual Prisons of Sexual Bondage

Justin was in a Prison of Sexual Bondage

Sadly, Justin was molested several times, at an early age, by a relative. He found himself perpetrating similar acts on younger boys. Justin turned to hard-core pornography and masturbation to satisfy his urges without hurting others. The more he looked at pornography, the more disgusted he was with himself. Here is Justin to share his prison experience.

> *I am bound by multiple ropes. I am contorted. My private parts have been torn off. There is a demon with a hot red poker shoving it into that space, burning it, constantly*

making it painful. I can smell the burning skin from the poker.

I am being forced to see crazy perverted images that I have never been attracted to, but I am feeling excited by them. I can't get any release. The demon holding the poker keeps turning it around in me; other demons are holding me back, making sure I am bound and hurting. I am forced to watch things. It is hot and unbearable.

I hear the sounds of screaming people. It's the sound of women being tortured around me. I hear a male voice behind me laughing, chuckling at what is going on. It is very hot and I am burning. There is a door in the distance. I know it's not real. It is false hope. It is too far to get to. I sense the real door is behind me. This is the door were the demons come in from. I'm forced to watch images of torture, porn, forced rapes. I'm forced to watch. I cannot turn away.

I ask Jesus to come in to get me out of the prison. As I do this, the colors change from a red, to a blue-metal room. It's like a hologram, but I'm still bound up. I am still trapped by the ropes and chains. As the ropes are cut away, my muscles are cramping from being held in that position for so long. I go out through the big door. I slam the door shut. I kick down and destroy the prison. I hand Jesus the piece of soul that was captured in that prison. It feels like a puffball or cotton ball. Jesus holds it between His fingers. It's now bright, clean, fresh and new. Jesus takes it and puts it into my chest. There is no trace of the holes in my groin. They are completely mended. I feel all new again.

I feel warm and soft and whole. I feel there was a place for that piece of soul that was missing. I now feel warm, relieved, in a good, safe place. I am safe now. The pain I was experiencing before is gone.

Jeremy's Prison Break from Sexual Bondage

Jeremy was exposed to pornography as a young boy by his grandfather. In his teens, Jeremy experimented with bondage situations, pornography, masturbation and group sex. He sought counseling to break the attraction of constant fleshly lust. But nothing would set him free. Jeremy agreed to ask Holy Spirit to show him the prison he might be in. Here is what Jeremy saw...

> *I see small cages, on a wall, on top of each other. I am in one of them. It is noisy, smells bad, and is dirty. I am lying on my side; it's very uncomfortable. People screaming, maybe I am too. I am naked, I feel shame, I feel horrible. Excruciating pain shoots into my head like bright sunshine in my eyes. I am not protected. I see really small dogs with huge teeth; they make a lot of noise...a hairy black creature jumps on my back, gnawing and scratching my back. A dark slimy demon holds a revolver. He is pointing it at me to make me afraid to get out.*
>
> *As soon as I could, I confessed and repented of my sins of lust. I desperately wanted to have a clean life from now on... without feeling guilty.*
>
> *I invited Jesus to come in and free me. Jesus took me out of prison. Jesus held my broken piece of soul in His hands. He blew on it and put it back in my chest. Jesus made me feel light and warm, like clean sheets.*

Jeremy was able to take his new-found freedom to higher levels. He was able to share his struggle with his wife and made himself accountable to an older Christian leader.

Matthew's Prison of Pornography

Many fine young men fall into the trap of pornography. Sometimes a family member or a friend exposes them to it, sometimes it just pops up on the Internet. The result is the same. The evil kingdom gains a legal right to take a piece of your soul and imprison it.

> *I am sitting in a wooden boat; it is small and fragile. I can't get out of it. It is on sticky, greasy liquid. I want to get out. I am a child. I can't swim. I can see scary faces in the dark liquid. The reflections scare me. I am sitting in wetness; it is dirty and smelly. I feel disgusted with myself because I am dirty with that slime. It is almost like oil on water. I can't scream. I feel helpless. I see a tiny island in the distance, like in a cartoon where the island has a coconut tree. The boat is far away from the island that is in the distance.*

I pledge allegiance to Jesus. Jesus leads me out of the prison. I give the imprisoned piece of my soul to Jesus.

I see silhouettes of angel faces and wings. I feel I am not dirty anymore. I feel peace.

Chapter 7

Spiritual Prisons of Voicelessness, Hopelessness, Death, Anxiety

Denise's Prison of Voicelessness

Denise had a father who abused her verbally. Nothing she ever did was right. Unknown to Denise, she was ripe for the demons to trap her into a prison of voicelessness. If you had met Denise, you would think she spoke up quite well. But Denise had a calling to be a leader and she was unable to step into that dimension.

> *...in this prison, my mouth is taped shut. The floor is made of molten lava rock. The walls are rock all around me, the ceiling is rock. It is very hot. I am wearing a pair of jogging shorts and a T-shirt. I have to keep jogging on the*

spot so my feet don't burn. I have no breath left to speak.

I am so glad that Holy Spirit is showing me this prison. I repent for judging and condemning my dad. I invite Jesus to come in and free me from this prison. Jesus comes immediately.

I am rejoicing that He is taking the bindings off of my arms. Jesus is loosening and untying the ropes. He is removing the tape from my mouth.

Jesus says, "Come with me. I'm going to take you up to the high places." Jesus is driving a two-seater convertible Lexus. The road in the mountains is going up. I receive freedom to go to higher heights, freedom in Jesus. It's a spiral road that we follow higher and higher. Jesus pardons me and He restores my eagle vision.

Denise not only received her voice but has helped other women to find their voices as she shares her story.

April's Prison Break from Hopelessness

April had a terrible time at school. She later learned that she was dyslexic, but her teachers did not know that when she was small. April was ridiculed by her teachers and classmates. She was kept in from recess to learn her alphabet. She was kept in at recess to learn math. One teacher threw her math book at her in class, in front of all the other students. Another teacher locked her into a closet. These traumatic events, among many others, robbed April of hope for the future.

Let's hear what kind of prison April found herself in.

> *I am in a place that has water coming from the ceiling, walls, and the floor. It is like I am in the middle of a washing machine. I am being thrown to and fro with no end in sight. I am treading water to keep my head above. I remember cursing myself saying, "I wished the world would stop."*
>
> *I break the curse. I invite Jesus to free me from this prison. I see Jesus swimming to me. He takes my hand. I am in front of Jesus. I finally feel calm, peace and life. He makes a bridge above the water; there is no wetness on the bridge.*
>
> *I give the piece of my broken soul to Jesus. I repent for feeling hopeless and not*

believing in Jesus to handle my life. I receive the blessing of trust.

I can see cracks in my soul. Jesus welds the cracks and removes the dirt. He puts a balm over my soul and covers it all over with a transparent liquid. Jesus says that I have to watch my thoughts.

As we talked with April, we could see a real change had taken place in her countenance. April has learned to look for the good in every circumstance which has helped her find joy in her everyday life.

Stacy's Prison Break from Death

The prison of death is diametrically opposed to the abundant life that God has designed for each of us. While Satan may be unable to kill us in the flesh, he and his demons are constantly looking for, and plotting scenarios to bring captives to a prison of death.

The prison of death includes excessive sadness, depression, suicidal thoughts, despair, and even sleep apnea. Let's hear how Stacy describes her experience with the prison of death.

I see a huge, vicious character in a helmet and a black robe. I see different images of me stuck in prison. In one, I am stuck on a wall, nailed to it.

In another, my head is trying to come out from underground and every time I get it out it's pushed back by a violent demon.

In another image, I see rats running around me. I see my hands tied with cords behind my back. I hear commotion. I can't see anything. I see a vision of fire. I'm being branded, burned in my right arm with a branding iron. Some kind of creature pinches my nose so I can't breathe.

I realize I need to confess and repent for my suicidal thoughts, despair, and sadness. Next, I call to Jesus to come and free me from this prison.

Jesus bursts on the scene. A bomb explodes at the entrance of the prison.

I can see the light outside; I can actually see the presence of an angel, taking me out, and untying me. There is light; I walk out of the prison led by the angel and I go through the door.

> *Jesus is also there. I give Jesus the piece of my soul. He says He has created me in His image… He wants me to decree His word. His word is life and power. I see Him putting His finger on my soul. Electricity is on it, like a fire on it. He puts it back inside my chest. I say, "Thank you Jesus. Joy and peace and abundant life are my birthright and come from You."*

Sometime later, Stacy gladly shared with us that she was spending more time reading the Bible and actually sharing the good news with her family and friends. We could see that Stacy was more vibrant and fully present in her newly discovered freedom.

Holly's Prison Break from Anxiety

Anxiety is often felt, but its causes are often hidden. Anxiety is closely related to fear. It may manifest in many different forms. Some forms are inward and passive such as—a lack of peace, lack of joy, insomnia, and bound emotions; while others are aggressive such as- panic attacks, speaking out loudly, easily irritated.

Holly's parents demanded perfection in everything she did. But Holly was never good enough to please them. Holly thought these feelings of anxiety would go away after she got married. She was wrong. She was always in fear of being criticized by her husband, even though he did not criticize her. Holly had no energy to do the things she liked. She could not sleep at night as her mind continually reviewed what she might have done wrong that day and what she had to do the next day. Holly finally sought out prayer ministry.

> *I see stairs, spiral stairs; I have to climb them, all the time, but I am not going anywhere, no matter what I do. I feel anxiety, frustration and a sense of worthlessness; nothing is going to change; I have to make more efforts... constant struggle with no change...I feel hopeless, I don't have any energy; waves of panic assault my soul over and over.*
>
> *I finally realize that I am not alone but that I have chosen to live life without the power of Jesus and Holy Spirit.*
>
> *I confess and repent for having put myself on the throne of my soul. I call out for Jesus to please come and free me from this prison and take His rightful place on the throne of my life.*
>
> *I see Jesus, and I see Holy Spirit in the form of a dove, flying towards me. Holy Spirit is touching my cheeks with His wings saying*

that I can rest on His wings. Wherever I go, I will always be supported.

I walk out of the prison with Jesus and close the door behind me.

The Lord is spraying dusty particles on my soul, covering it with white powder, then with gold powder. I say, "Thank you Jesus."

I choose to believe that I have peace with Jesus and lots of energy and dunamis power from Holy Spirit. I am refusing to be held captive by anxiety any more. In the future, when I feel anxiety, I will identify the problem and give it to Jesus.... and not take it back.

Holly reported that she was developing the habit of taking every problem in her life to Jesus. Each time she would feel lighter and better able to cope with life.

Chapter 8

Spiritual Prisons of Sugar, Self, Neglect, Jealousy, Rebellion

Laura's Prison Break from Sugar

(We had heard of the demon of sugar and the demon of chocolate, but this was our first encounter with the prison of sugar.)

Laura was an attractive lady in her early 40s. She appeared fit and healthy. It came as a shock to her and to us that Holy Spirit showed her that she was in a prison of sugar.

> *Holy Spirit tells me I am in a prison of sugar. I see myself dressed in a black, full length leotard, drowning in an ocean of white sugar.*

There appears to be a whirlpool in the middle of the ocean of sugar. I am at the edge of the whirlpool, facing away from the center, and swimming as fast as I can to keep myself from being swallowed by the whirlpool in the ocean of sugar. I am always out of breath, but I eventually utter a weak scream for Jesus to save me.

Suddenly, I'm on a floating air mattress, above tons of sugar, not touching the sugar. Jesus is pulling me with a cord. It looks like I am on a sled going over the snow, but actually I am sliding over sugar. We finally reach the shore. I can now stand and breathe normally. Jesus leads me out of the prison of sugar.

Laura had always found it strange that she was unable to stop herself from eating sugary foods. After her prison break Laura found it much easier to avoid eating sugar.

Robert's Prison Break from the Prison of Self

Most of us, if we cared to admit it, are always thinking about how we can make ourselves happier, wealthier, and more popular. While some of the time, we do think of others, it's because it brings us pleasure to be with them or to give them gifts. Jesus wants us to focus our attention on Him. Then the Father can give us the desires of our hearts. Here is how Robert experienced his prison of self.

> *I am in some kind of Spiritual Prison. I am wrapped up in cords.... big cords, thin cords, colored ones, old ones. My arms and legs are wrapped tightly. I looked like an Egyptian mummy, although my head was free.*
>
> *I am able to hop, although my arms are tied up. I am still trying to do stuff on my own. I am so focused on all the cords. I am trying to eat with no hands. Holy Spirit tells me that I am in a prison of self, because I'm trying to live my life under my own power. Holy Spirit says I am doing many good things, but I have to learn to lean on Jesus and use His power.*
>
> *I hear Jesus calling me to focus. Jesus says to look at him, so all self will disappear. By trusting in Him, all the cords of self will come off.*
>
> *Next, I see Jesus unwrapping the white cords and folding them in a bowl. He is telling me to look at Him. He is saying that I am now free.*

> *I see my feet in a bucket. There is goop all over. I am confused. Jesus says, "I need to cleanse your past and make your way straight."*

In commenting on the ministry later, Robert said, "I already feel a new freedom singing inside me. There is more energy surging inside of me. I love this ministry."

The Spiritual Prison of Neglect

In this type of prison, the prisoner is truly a victim of injustice. In most of the Spiritual Prisons we see, the prisoner has erred in some way, giving legal rights to the evil kingdom to incarcerate a piece of their soul. In the prison of neglect, the child may be the victim of uncaring parents, or cruel realities of life, such as early death of their parents.

Erin's Prison Break from Neglect.

> *I am in a prison of cold. It is in an ice castle. It is a prison of lack of love from my parents and family. There is tension. I see a little girl about age 10 to 12, frozen stiff, sitting on a block of ice. She is cold and lonely, neglected,*

not wanted, not appreciated... love is outside; warmth is outside. The frozen little girl is me.

I ask Jesus to come and melt the ice, to free me from this prison. I see flames of fire melting the ice that is surrounding me.

Instantly, I realize that this prison has been preventing me from experiencing the fiery love of Jesus. I believe and receive the truth that this ice prison has been demolished and the entire issue of neglect has been dealt with.

Erin's friends shared with us that they could see a real change in Erin after her ministry time. They said that somehow she seems more on fire for God.

Valerie's Prison of Jealousy

Valerie not only learned jealousy from her parents; she took it to new extremes. She always had to have the latest gadgets, the finest clothes, the coolest boyfriends. Valerie spent all her time comparing herself with others. She was afraid to let people see her real self because her real self might be rejected. As long as Valerie had better stuff than others, they would have to like her... or so she thought.

In Valerie's prison, she was prevented from acquiring anything. But because Valerie was a Christian already, she was able to keep a pair of gold shoes, even in the prison, perhaps because she was the daughter of the Most High God. Valerie was really unaware of her powerful position as a daughter of God. The demons constantly soiled her gold shoes to prevent her from walking in her inheritance.

> *I am in an open area, surrounded by ugly creatures that mock me and will not let me out of their circle. They keep saying that there is no way to get out...that I am a loser, no one likes me, I am all alone. Whenever I walk they walk with me, keeping me in the center of them like a hub in a wheel. I am wearing solid gold shoes. The demons keep throwing mud onto my shoes, trying to make them look like muddy, rubber boots. But my golden shoes keep on glowing. I don't know why. I feel trapped. It is hard to see what else is around because the ugly creatures are in the way.*
>
> *I confess and repent for not being thankful for all God has given me and for being jealous of other people. I invite Jesus to come into this prison and to free me.*

> *Jesus blasts with the sound of a shofar, the piece of soul that had been in the prison, and frees me. All the dust and dirt blow off. I feel renewed, loved and accepted.*

Valerie told us a few months later that she was seeing herself more as God sees her. She was able to reduce the frequency of comparing herself to others. She also was alert to jealousy and its subtle tricks.

Jennifer's Prison Break from Rebellion

Jennifer was the last child in a family of five children. It seemed that everyone, brothers and sisters, believed they could tell Jennifer what to do. Her mother was very controlling, as was her father. There was no room for her to think for herself and besides Jennifer could never do anything right in their eyes. So eventually, when she reached 16, Jennifer opened the door to the demon of rebellion and subsequently became an inmate in a Spiritual Prison of rebellion. Jennifer was mad at God, herself and well, just about everyone. Let's hear how she describes her prison.

> *I see walls with spikes in them. The spikes seem to have voices, constantly telling me what I can and cannot do. The floor is moving.*

I am thrown from one side to the other while trying to stand up in this prison. I have a spear in my hand. The spear makes me think I am in control, but in reality it is useless.

I see pairs of eyes above the many spikes. The eyes behind the spikes are ready to attack me at any time. They are judging and accusing me of not measuring up.

A beam of light comes from time to time and crosses the room. Later, Jesus tells me that it was Him coming by to see if I was ready get out of prison.

I am hearing sounds like a low buzz. It starts and stops. There is a mucky substance on the ground, like wet mud. The spikes are attacking me. I feel attacked from every side. Rebellion is my only control.

Jesus comes in as a radiant person dressed in white robes. He takes the spear out of my hand. I walk out of prison.

I give Jesus a piece of my soul that was stuck in the prison.

Jesus says that I have a special place in my heart for you.

He wipes my soul clean and put it back in my chest.

I feel good.

My ministers led me to see that I was holding onto an ungodly belief, "I must rebel to be safe." After I confessed and repented for this ungodly belief and embraced the new godly belief that "God is my protection," I received the blessing of humility.

Jennifer reported that she was learning every day to be more in the presence of Jesus and it was helping her to be at peace in different kinds of situations.

CHAPTER 9

Testimonies

Testimony from Heather About a Prison Break from Self-condemnation

Dear Bruce and Evelyne,

Thank You so much for your prayers. The way I used to feel, was that people did not like me nor want my ideas. I sense that God has set me free from that prison that I have been in for so long. Since you prayed for me I have NOT had those thoughts.

Yesterday, I was sitting in Church. I had been asked before if I would tell about hearing God's voice. But during the week, my pastor said that he had changed the sermon and wanted to have me speak the following week. As I sat in church, some of the old thinking crept in, such as: "Ohh he did NOT want you. Look at you! The way you are talking is not good enough..." Many condemning thoughts....

Right away I was aware of how destroying those thoughts were and I was able to pray and ask God to stop them, and to tell me the truth. So I sense that I am growing in this new freedom in Christ. Thank you again for your prayers.

God's blessings on You.
Heather

Richard's Testimonies About His Multiple Prison Breaks

Richard came to us to be healed from the damaging effects of growing up in an alcoholic home, to be emotionally healed from long-standing childhood wounds, and to be delivered from demonic oppression.

Richard had been abused by his dad, his whole life. His mom blamed him, his siblings rejected him, other kids bullied him, church leaders rejected him, his wife rejected him and he got divorced.

His basic belief became 'I don't matter.' Richard projected his father's image onto God resulting in distrust and distance.

His father was very angry, both verbally and emotionally abusive. Richard had a very dependent type relationship with him. As a third child, he was not wanted. He was sometimes dishonest with himself, and very passive.

Richard had trouble speaking. He had felt the weight of the abuse on his back, literally feeling muscle aches and pains all over. He had been abandoned and neglected.

He felt depressed and hopeless, alone and voiceless. He became jealous of others, stuffing bitterness and anger deep down inside. His rebellion showed itself in mistrust of other people. Because he experienced grief over the way life was turning out, he turned to masturbation and sexual bondage thinking they would bring relief.

Self-hate started to rule his life. Depression followed and then accidents, sickness, and being fired from work. Adding to the weight was the false responsibility he had with his father. In order to matter, Richard believed he had to try to please his father, even though he never could.

He lived all of his life in shame. Richard's prisons included self-rejection, self-hate, self-loathing, some occult bondage, sadness and depression, anger towards his father, anger towards himself, shame, fear, and voicelessness. This oppression felt like carrying a big weight on his back.

Richard saw himself in a prison with his hands tied behind his back, his head hanging down, with a look of hopelessness, and being totally tied up with many cords. Richard saw it this way...

> *I can only move my head.*
>
> *A huge demon, the jail master, is standing over me to my right side. Behind me, many other shadows, not clear, are all looking down at me.*
>
> *I am wearing a black robe as if I am dead.*
>
> *I see scars on my face and chest, bruises bleeding all over my body. The whole place is quite dark and has a bad smell all around. I am starving without food.*
>
> *I can feel physical pain. I want to cry but I can't and don't have the strength or hope... I'll be in this prison forever.*
>
> *I desperately want to break out of this prison, so I ask Holy Spirit how to get out of here? He tells me the key is forgiveness. I agree to forgive my dad.*
>
> *Beams of light come in, the light of God. Demons are stepping back. It feels like the*

chains are falling off. I see myself covered in the light of Christ.

I'm raising my hands, thanking God for what He did. I'm telling Jesus I belong to Him forever. I see angels rejoicing; chains are gone; nothing is binding me. The glory of God is on my face. I feel wonderful, free. Jesus is looking down at me, smiling. I say, "Thank You, Jesus."

Jesus is holding His hands out to me, saying, "You are welcome."

I see angels take me up to Jesus, presenting me. He is holding me up straight, looking into my eyes. I am totally covered by His love. He is saying that everything He promised in my dreams will come to pass. I see Him put His hand on me, blessing me, saying, "Go and do the works I have called you to do."

I see myself coming back, walking on earth, giving thanks to God.

The next day at work, I was calmer and focused. I worked better. It was not a struggle like before. I seemed to have more time. I listened to the audio clips of my prison break that you emailed me. My body was lighter, not bound, nor restricted.

I still have some tensions remaining- in that I am coming out of prison for the first time. I have been a stranger to myself all my life.

Now I can look at myself in the mirror; I hated myself so much before.

Richard called us a few weeks after.

He told us he had more time, more energy, that he read the Bible better, had more peace, felt more freedom, could concentrate better, had so many breakthroughs, the depression was broken off, and that he was looking forward to life…

I don't feel trapped anymore; I am making progress. I'm in control more.

I'm in the light for the first time. I'm free to talk with Jesus, enjoying fellowship with Him. Fear and shame have left; there is no condemnation anymore. I can look at Jesus' face for the first time with no fear. I was in jail all my life but now I am free to go and do what I want. This is a day I've been waiting for, for so long.

I have a very clear mind; the darts now bounce off of me. I can breathe; new life has come back and I feel lighter. The muscle aches are gone and my throat is clear; the tiredness has gone...

The tension is gone, I have freedom to move my body now. I feel whole again, in one piece.

Richard's comment on the evaluation sheet:

I also received a special ministry time during which I was set free from a lifetime of being trapped inside a prison... the ministry flowed under the leading of Holy Spirit and was, as you can see, very effective.

Angela's Testimony

Angela comments:
1) How was I before? As far as I remember, I was very often ashamed of my person and character, and regularly felt not being "good enough."

2) What happened in my vision? I was in a closed room/cell deep in the earth with no connection to the surface.

Let's listen as Angela shares her story.

I was in a cell under the earth, way, way down, where there was lava. It was very hot. No one can hear me when I scream.

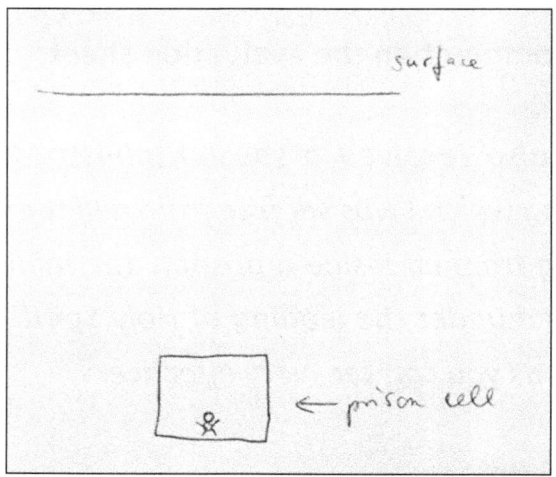

There were worms. The worms were ugly like the worms eating through an apple, but much bigger. I feel I will never get out. I am terrified. I am pushing the earth behind me. I have tried to dig out a tunnel, but failed. I fall back, very exhausted. I see me in the act of falling out of the air onto the floor being slammed, over and over. I'm running against a wall, a gummy wall. I am being thrown against the walls. I'm lying on the floor,

exhausted. Someone, a creature, is whacking me with a huge carpet beater, blaming me, being mean to me without reason. I am on the floor, thinking this is horrible. I hate to be beaten like that. I try to protect myself holding my arms/hands above my head. I am sitting on the floor. Suddenly, a giant snake rolls out. It slides over me. The snake oozed a colorful but painful slime on me. My arms are burning from this slime. It is a horrible torture. I scream and scream.

Then, I ask Jesus to get me out of this prison. In a flash, there was a kind of a giant drill coming down from the surface making a tunnel towards me.

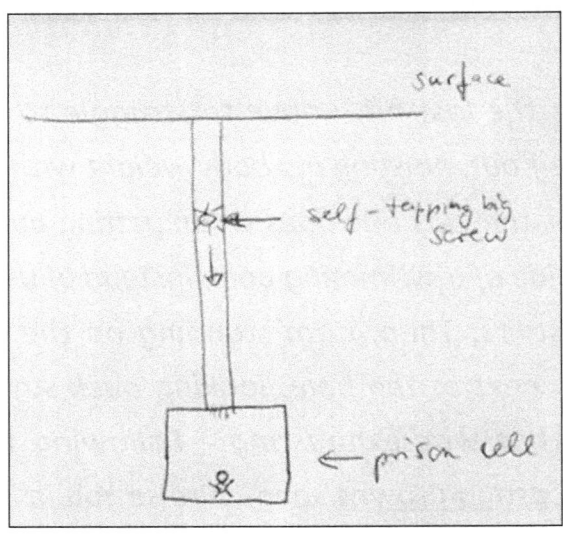

Getting to the surface was then easy as I was standing on the earth as sand/earth was going into the cell from the bottom lifting me up gradually.

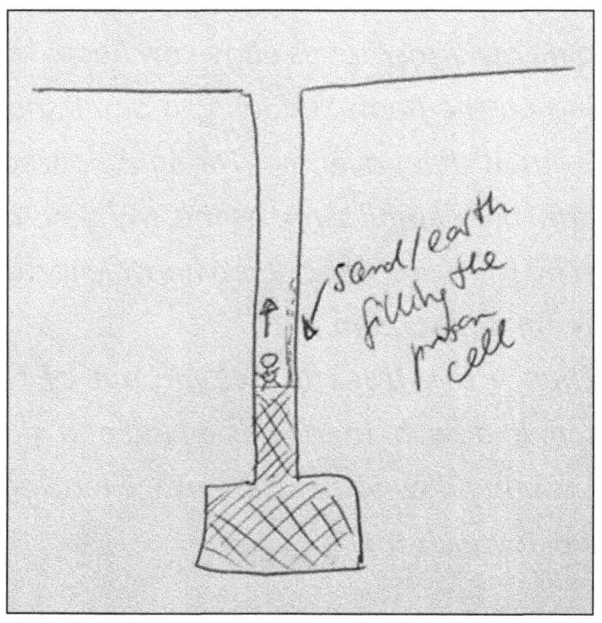

In the last bit, I have to struggle to get myself out, hoisting my body weight with my arms, the way one does when getting out at the side of a swimming pool, instead of using the stairs. Then, I am standing on the surface, next to the hole, looking back saying, "Oh that was exhausting!" Following this, the <u>Casting Crowns</u> song, "Praise You in This

Storm" comes to my mind as a thunderstorm came up. I am not worried at all as I know I am out of the prison, and my dirt would be washed off.

I ask Jesus to wash me; to wash the dirt off. I ask Jesus to heal my heart.

I see my big heart filled with lava; it was like Holy Spirit came down as a dove, and then the water came down. The outside would become stone, so the inner heart would be protected by the outer part which had cooled a little *and become harder. Afterwards, I saw myself lying in a beach chair wearing sunglasses to protect myself from the sun... finally relaxing... thank you Jesus*

Authors' note: Angela saw healthy protection of her heart with the outside "lava cooling to stone" and keeping her inner heart warm and soft always.

I am very pleased that I rarely feel "not good enough" anymore!
I consider myself more able to be GOD's daughter and therefore I am entitled to be and also do what He has created me for! I really have this joy in revisiting how Jesus freed me from this prison.
I am now able to claim my freedom from shame and unworthiness "consciously"!

Praise GOD! Amen.

Chapter 10

Spiritual Prison Break Ministry Procedure

The following outlines how we do a Spiritual Prison Break. We bring these revelations humbly before you. There may be others with similar revelation but we don't know about them. We bless you to use what we have been shown by Holy Spirit. If you have any suggestions based on your use of our approach, please let us know.

If you are already a pastor, or prayer minister, and would like to use our method, we recommend that you have a ministering partner. We encourage you to have intercessors providing prayer covering, to listen with your spirit, and operate out of deep love for God and the client. In some cases, it may be necessary for both of you and the client to fast. Use a private place to do the session.

Prior to a prison break session, the client needs to have had sessions with the ministers to spiritually clean up his/her past hurts, ungodly beliefs, ungodly identities, soul ties, generational iniquities, etc. The client needs to forgive everyone he/she has not yet fully forgiven (including repenting for judgments.) We encourage the ministers to complete the preparatory work and not just jump into a prison break. No two prison breaks are the same, so it is important to let Holy Spirit do the leading.

We ask God to send ministering angels and warrior angels to assist. Their presence and the presence of Jesus protect us from demons. Tell the client to keep his/her eyes closed during the session. Again, we recommend that the person ministering has someone else helping, praying in tongues, and listening to Holy Spirit…Tell the client to ask Holy Spirit to show him/her the prison He wants to free him/her from.

Ask the client to begin to sense what *Holy Spirit* is revealing to him/her.

Say, "Be sure to explain to us the position you are in and what is going on around you. Slowly let the Holy Spirit reveal more and more details, sights, sounds, smells, pains, shackles if any, activity, senses." (Do not tell the client about your visions and what you are sensing, no matter how vivid. This would interfere with what *Holy Spirit* is doing.)

Say to the client, "Ask Jesus to join you in this prison. When you sense His presence, declare your allegiance to Jesus as Lord and Savior and that in His name and by your authority in Him as a believer, the chains of hell cannot bind you. Declare your freedom in the name of Jesus."

Jesus is the key that opens the prison door. He usually leads the person out of the prison, but sometimes He may use angels. The client, keeping their eyes closed, needs to physically get up and walk out of the prison with the help of the minister. The prison door needs to be closed by the client because what we say and do prophetically impacts both kingdoms.

Does the Client Need to be a Believer in Jesus, God and Holy Spirit to Get Out of a Spiritual Prison?

Technically NO, Jesus can free anyone anytime He wants.

If you have read this entire book, you will appreciate just how much Jesus wants people to be free from the lies of the evil kingdom. You should also have seen that *Holy Spirit* reveals the Spiritual Prison the person is in, so Jesus can come and free him/her. You probably concluded that God really loves us. Chances are this is new information for you. If so, you need to make a decision. If you want Jesus in your life here are some words to say to invite Him into your heart:

> *God I can see you are pure goodness. I see I am loved by You. I am sorry for all the things I have done wrong in my life. I believe Jesus died for my sins so I can have eternal life and belong to Your family. I ask You Jesus, Son of God, to be the leader of my life and heart and fill me with the power of Your Holy Spirit.*

If you said these words and meant them, you are now a newly born child into the family of God. Congratulations. If you will send us an email, we will pray for you. ***youaregodschosen@gmail.com***

Why Should People Do a Prison Break Session?

Not everyone will need a prison break. But some will have different kinds of prisons, and so may need two or three Spiritual Prison break sessions. Once freed, the client needs to be careful to avoid falling into their old patterns of behavior and thinking, and consequently allowing himself/herself to be imprisoned again.

Each of us is a necessary part of the Body of the Church, the Bride of Christ. We need to be whole and clean in order to reign with Jesus, bringing heaven to earth. We are meant to govern at the end, and we need to be cleaned up to govern; we need to become more like Christ. We don't want to leave any parts of our souls trapped in Satanic Spiritual Prisons.

May God bless you in your journey!

APPENDIX

Bible verses referring to Spiritual Prisons

I waited patiently for the Lord; he turned to me and heard my cry. He lifted me out of the slimy pit, out of the mud and mire...
Psalm 40: 1,2 NIV

Was David really in a slimy pit that he couldn't get out of in the physical? Or was David referring to a Spiritual Prison?

He brought them out of darkness, the utter darkness,
    and broke away their chains.
Let them give thanks to the LORD for his unfailing love
    and his wonderful deeds for mankind,

> for he breaks down gates of bronze
> > and cuts through bars of iron.
> > Psalm 107: 10-16 NIV

We can see that the prisoners are suffering because of sinning against God. Utter darkness refers to a place without God. The gates of bronze and iron are prophetic words to describe Spiritual Prisons that Jesus will destroy.

> Rescue me from the mire,
> > do not let me sink;
> > deliver me from those who hate me,
> > from the deep waters.
> > Do not let the floodwaters engulf me
> > or the depths swallow me up
> > or the pit close its mouth over me.
> > Psalm 69: 14,15 NIV

David talks here in prophetic terms about the pit, floodwaters, the depths. David's body is not in an actual pit surrounded by mud with floodwaters immersing him, but it is his soul that is experiencing these challenges, from which only God can save him.

> [18] The Spirit of the Lord is upon me, because he hath anointed me to preach the gospel to

> the poor; he hath sent me to heal the brokenhearted, to preach deliverance to the captives, and recovering of sight to the blind, to set at liberty them that are bruised, Luke 4: 18 KJV

If Jesus is to "preach deliverance to the captives," then where might the captives be if not in a Spiritual Prison?

When Jesus began His ministry, He quoted Isaiah 61:1,2. Most Christians are very familiar with this passage. Jesus did not set up a ministry to free prisoners from physical jails. So how did He proclaim freedom for the prisoners? He delivered people from the kingdom of darkness, which includes Spiritual Prisons. He gave this authority to all of His believers.

> Jesus called his twelve disciples to him and gave them authority to drive out impure spirits and to heal every disease and sickness. Matthew 10:1 NIV

> I have given you authority to trample on snakes and scorpions and to overcome all the power of the enemy; Luke 10:19 NIV

We believe it is our mandate as followers of Jesus to go and free our brothers and sisters from Spiritual Prisons.

www.ingramcontent.com/pod-product-compliance
Ingram Content Group UK Ltd.
Pitfield, Milton Keynes, MK11 3LW, UK
UKHW022223230426
12048UKWH00016BA/1029